To my mother, Tanya H. Russell (1938-2014),
who said many times, with a twinkle in her eye, that she
would know she had "died and gone to heaven" if she could sing
backup for Aretha. I have vivid, warm memories of us singing
Aretha's songs together—at the top of our lungs.
—K. R-B.

For Roberta,
fabulous in every way.
A great singer, a wonderful sister, and an even better friend.
My very own Diva.
—L. F.

BLOOMSBURY CHILDREN'S BOOKS
Bloomsbury Publishing Inc., part of Bloomsbury Publishing Plc
1385 Broadway, New York, NY 10018

BLOOMSBURY, BLOOMSBURY CHILDREN'S BOOKS, and the Diana logo are trademarks of Bloomsbury Publishing Plc

First published in the United States of America in January 2020
by Bloomsbury Children's Books

Text copyright © 2020 by Katheryn Russell-Brown • Illustrations copyright © 2020 by Laura Freeman

Bloomsbury books may be purchased for business or promotional use. For information on bulk purchases please contact
Macmillan Corporate and Premium Sales Department at specialmarkets@macmillan.com

Library of Congress Cataloging-in-Publication Data
Names: Russell-Brown, Katheryn, author. | Freeman, Laura (Illustrator) illustrator.
Title: A voice named Aretha / by Katheryn Russell-Brown ; illustrated by Laura Freeman.
Description: New York : Bloomsbury Children's Books, 2020.
Identifiers: LCCN 2019019149 (print) | LCCN 2019021877 (e-book)
ISBN 978-1-68119-850-7 (hardcover) • ISBN 978-1-5476-0273-5 (e-book) • ISBN 978-1-5476-0274-2 (e-PDF)
Subjects: LCSH: Franklin, Aretha—Juvenile literature. | Soul musicians—United States—Biography. |
African American singers—Biography—Juvenile literature. | Singers—United States—Biography—Juvenile literature.
Classification: LCC ML3930.F68 R87 2020 (print) | LCC ML3930.F68 (e-book) | DDC 782.421644092 [B] —dc23
LC record available at https://lccn.loc.gov/2019019149

Art created digitally with Photoshop • Book design by John Candell • Typeset in Mentor and HenHouse
Printed in China by Leo Paper Products, Heshan, Guangdong
2 4 6 8 10 9 7 5 3 1

All papers used by Bloomsbury Publishing Plc are natural, recyclable products made from wood grown in well-managed forests.
The manufacturing processes conform to the environmental regulations of the country of origin.

To find out more about our authors and books visit www.bloomsbury.com and sign up for our newsletters.

A Voice Named Aretha

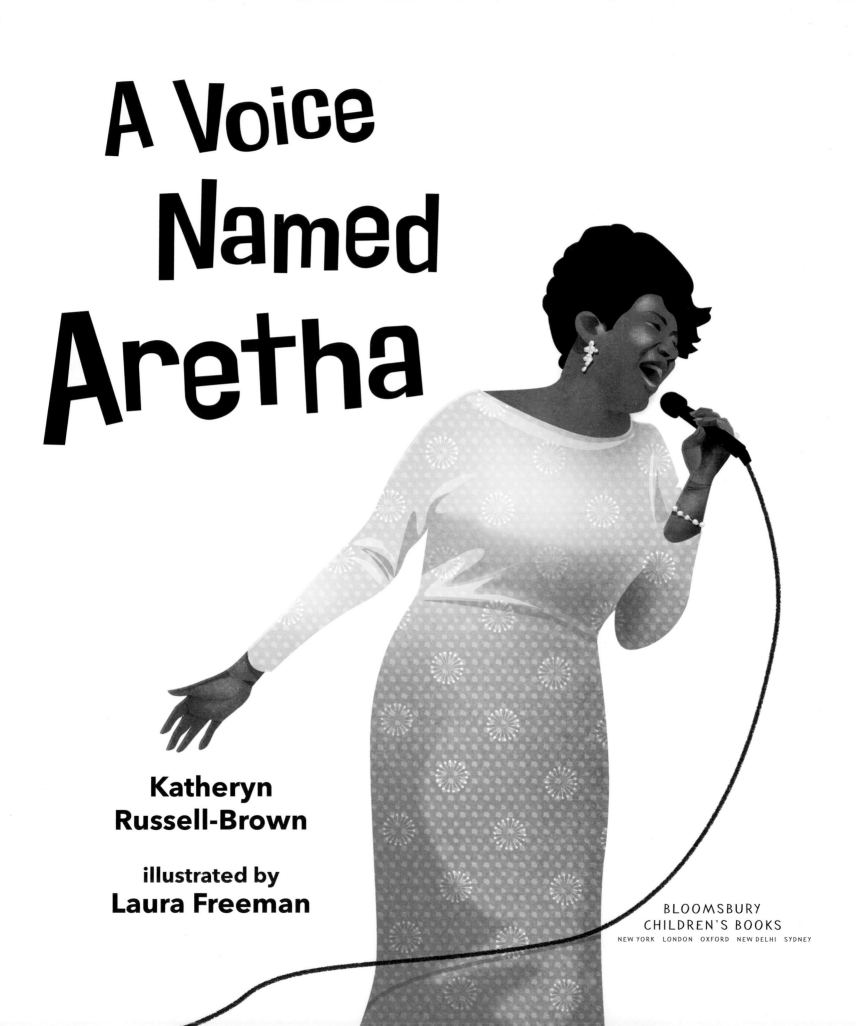

Katheryn Russell-Brown

illustrated by Laura Freeman

BLOOMSBURY
CHILDREN'S BOOKS
NEW YORK LONDON OXFORD NEW DELHI SYDNEY

Folks came from miles around to hear Reverend C. L. Franklin preach at New Bethel Baptist Church in Detroit, Michigan. The famous preacher gave soul-stirring sermons that could make you shout, moan, or nod and whisper "Amen."

The Franklins' big brick house was always brimming with people. And music. Everybody who was anybody, in music and civil rights, visited the Franklin home: Ella Fitzgerald, Duke Ellington, Dinah Washington, and Nat King Cole. Dr. Martin Luther King Jr. was a close friend and a regular guest.

It was in this house, full of talking, singing, and organizing, that a shy little girl named Aretha Louise Franklin grew up.

Aretha and her brothers and sisters loved singing in church, clapping along with the organ, drums, and tambourines. Each young Franklin wanted to shine bright for Daddy.

Little Aretha had the biggest voice of all. She sang soulful trills and powerful riffs with a deep, easy feeling, well beyond her years. No doubt about it, Aretha was the star child.

When Mother Barbara and Daddy Franklin's marriage ended, Mother moved back to Buffalo, New York. The children stayed with their father and visited their mother every summer.

Quiet Aretha missed her mother dearly, but she enjoyed watching her care for patients at the hospital where she worked. She cherished the nurse's kit Mother gave her.

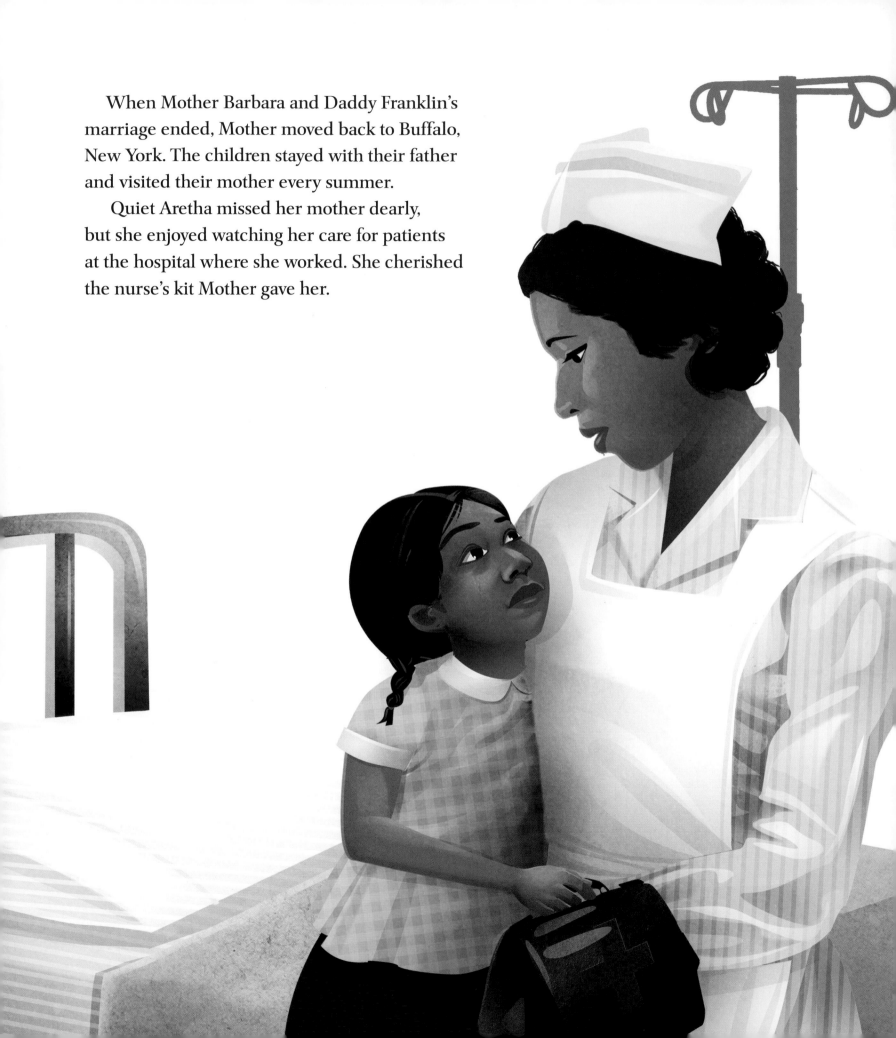

But in 1952, right before Aretha turned ten, something very sad happened. Her mother passed away. Part of Aretha's heart died right along with Mother Barbara.

A few months later, Aretha practiced to sing her first church solo. The week before her performance, she was a bundle of nerves and tears.

When the day came, she stood on a chair and belted out "Jesus Be a Fence Around Me." More than a thousand people heard Aretha sing that beautiful, uplifting song. At only ten years old, she figured out a way to draw strength from her sadness.

Music was Aretha's calling: Singing it and playing it.
She spent hours listening to rhythm & blues, gospel,
and jazz records, letting the words and melodies
take her imagination to exciting new places. With
her uncanny ear for music, when Aretha heard
someone sing a tune or play a song on the
piano, she could sing it or play it right
back, just like that.

Twelve-year-old Aretha joined the Gospel
Caravan, Daddy Franklin's traveling ministry.
Church folks from California to North Carolina
marveled at the young girl with the voice of
an old soul. Just like her daddy's preaching,
Aretha's singing could move people to jump up,
sway, and hum along.

By age eighteen, Aretha was ready to share her talent with the world. She moved to the Big Apple, where she and Daddy Franklin met with Phil Moore, a famous voice coach. After hearing her sing and play the piano, he was an instant fan.

"I can't take your money," he told Daddy Franklin. He could see that Aretha already had her own musical style.

Before long, Aretha had signed a deal with a top record company.

Aretha was a songbird ready to fly.

The 1960s were a turbulent time. By law, whites and blacks were separated—in schools, churches, libraries, swimming pools, even graveyards. People wanted change. They marched in the streets, demanding jobs, racial equality, and an end to the Vietnam War.

Aretha paid close attention to the news. She knew that separate meant unequal and refused to perform for "whites only" audiences. Aretha sang only where people of all races could attend. She stayed true to what she learned as a child—that every person deserves fair treatment.

Before she went on tour with her band, Aretha was warned that club owners sometimes tricked singers out of their money. No way was she going to let that happen! She demanded payment in cash, before the show. And when she went on stage, she always put her handbag where she could see it. Aretha could put on a show *and* take care of business.

Although the crowds loved her, Aretha's albums flopped. She had worked too hard to let her talent go to waste. She had to do something big.

She got a new band and signed on with a new record company. And finally . . . a smash hit! "I Never Loved a Man (The Way I Love You)" sold more than a million records. A few months later, her sing-along classic "Respect" was released. Then came the icing on the cake when Aretha was crowned the "Queen of Soul." At last, she had found her groove.

Aretha wasn't afraid of hard work.

Seeing the Queen of Soul perform was an experience to remember, and in 1987, her lifetime of music was celebrated when she was the first woman voted into the Rock & Roll Hall of Fame.

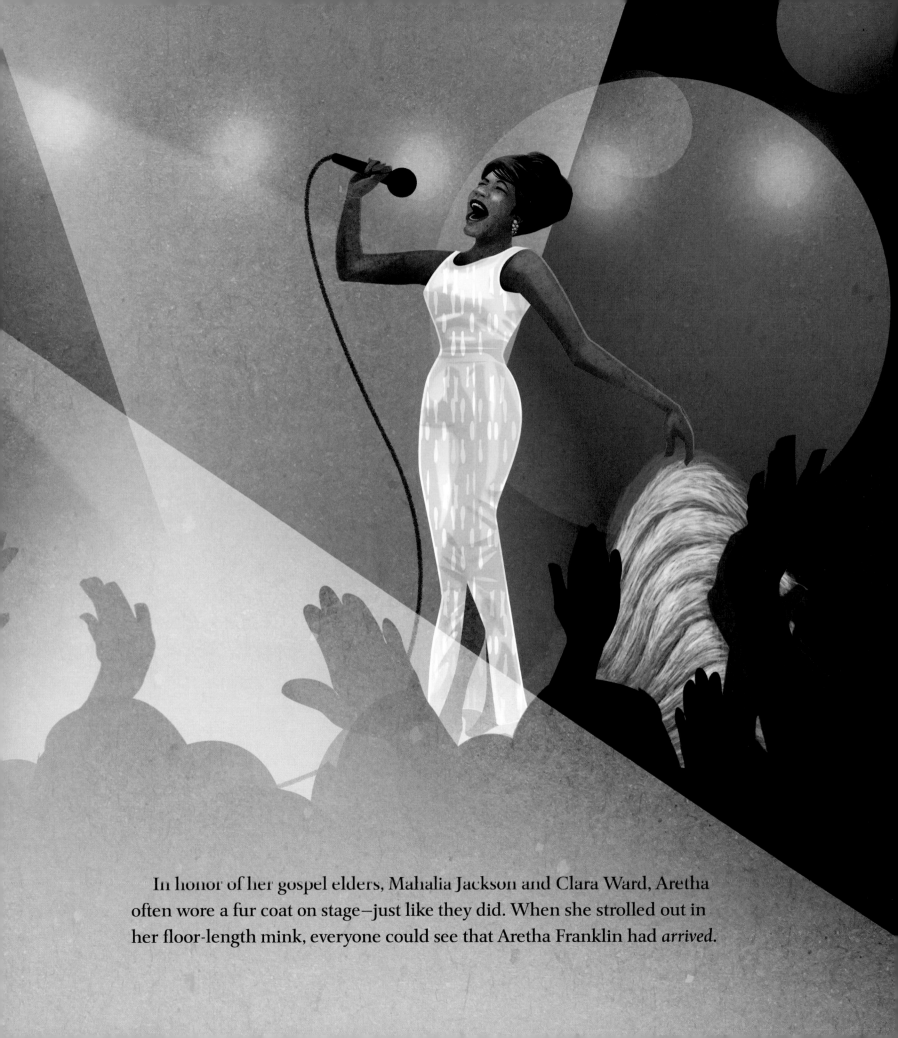

In honor of her gospel elders, Mahalia Jackson and Clara Ward, Aretha often wore a fur coat on stage—just like they did. When she strolled out in her floor-length mink, everyone could see that Aretha Franklin had *arrived*.

Aretha kept singing through the sweet spots and the rough patches of her life. She learned that hit songs did not always guarantee love or happiness. Some of the men Aretha fell in love with were as good as gold. A few were not so nice. In time, she learned to demand a little respect from everybody.

Aretha's music didn't just soothe her pain, it inspired black people, women, and people of all colors to stand up for justice. Whenever she performed, Aretha left the crowd with a soulful memory.

Aretha used her voice as a helping hand. When opera singer Luciano Pavarotti got sick before a performance, Aretha put her music skills to work. She had twenty minutes to learn "Nessun Dorma" before going on stage. TV audiences around the globe saw her masterful performance—she sang in English and in Italian.

Since high school, Aretha donated money to people and businesses in Detroit. She also performed in lots of concerts to raise money for civil rights groups. Aretha used her voice to make people feel good and to make the world a better place.

Aretha's voice had magic tucked inside. And that magic could work a spell. Sometimes the spell brings people to tears— even the president of the United States.

Each one of her songs is like a sermon, with a story and a lesson, seasoned with life wisdom, hard work, and always, lots of soul. They remind us of the greatest joy or the deepest pain.

The shy girl who sang with a broken heart set her sights high and became a confident, singing powerhouse. Aretha believed in her gift and dared us to believe in it too. Her songs inspire us to think, love, and respect ourselves and one another.

When we hear her sing, we can thank our lucky stars that our ears crossed paths with a voice named Aretha.

MORE ABOUT THE QUEEN OF SOUL

Aretha Louise Franklin was born on March 25, 1942, in Memphis, Tennessee. Her parents, Barbara Siggers and C. L. Franklin, had four children together, Erma, Cecil, Aretha, and Carolyn. When they married, Barbara Siggers already had a young son, Vaughn. C. L. Franklin was a minister, and the family moved as new opportunities arose for him. Siggers, who sang and played the piano, worked as a nurse's aide. In 1944, the family moved to Buffalo, where Reverend Franklin was a pastor at Friendship Baptist Church. Two years later, they moved to Detroit after Reverend Franklin was selected to lead New Bethel Baptist Church. The Franklins moved into the large, six-bedroom parsonage home. Aretha said she felt "like a fairy-tale princess living in a castle."

Each of the Franklin children sang gospel music. Each one was talented. It was clear early on, however, that Aretha had something special. Smokey Robinson, who was a childhood friend of Aretha's brother Cecil, said that her gift was obvious at a young age: "'She came from a distant musical planet where children are born with their gifts fully formed.'"

When the Franklins' marriage ended, Barbara Siggers moved to Buffalo with Vaughn. Aretha and her siblings were devastated, Aretha particularly so. She cried for days after her mother moved more than 200 miles away. In anticipation of her trips to visit her mother, Aretha would pack her suitcase days early. Sadly, in 1952, just before Aretha turned ten, her mother died of a heart attack. Aretha was inconsolable. Not long after losing her mother, Aretha sang her first church solo, "Jesus Be a Fence Around Me." The parishioners were spellbound by her mature and emotional voice.

Many people stepped in to help Reverend Franklin raise his children, including his mother, Rachel Franklin, known as "Big Mama," gospel singers Clara Ward and Mahalia Jackson, and a friend, Lola Moore. Among other things, these women taught Aretha how to cook soul food.

Growing up, Aretha met many famous members of the black community in her living room. Reverend Franklin, a nationally known pastor and community activist, was friends with leaders in the Civil Rights Movement, including Dr. Martin Luther King Jr., a close family friend. Aretha grew up listening to conversations, meetings, and strategy sessions on how to improve the lives of black Americans.

At the age of twelve, Aretha joined her father's traveling gospel caravan. They toured cities around the country. The shows featured gospel music's biggest acts, including Mahalia Jackson, Albertina Walker, Sam Cooke & the Soul Stirrers, and the Caravans. They performed at churches, fairs, theaters, and gospel conventions.

Songs of Faith, Aretha's first album, was recorded when she was just fourteen. The album is a live recording of Aretha singing at her father's church. By then, she was already a local legend. When Berry Gordy Jr.—who later founded Motown Records—heard her sing at New Bethel Baptist, he and his writing partner (Billy "Roquel" Davis), tried to sign young Aretha to their label. Reverend Franklin did not give his permission because he felt she was too young to join the music industry.

Aretha's talent continued to develop, and by the time she was eighteen, Reverend Franklin agreed that she was ready to move to New York City and to transition from gospel to secular music. In 1960, Aretha signed with Columbia Records. Unfortunately, her time there was frustrating. She released several albums, but none had any breakout hits. Her 1966 move to Atlantic Records was the perfect fit. The magic began with her first song, "I Never Loved a Man (The Way I Love You)," which sold more than one million copies and immediately cemented her as a

contender. She had a legendary musical partnership with producer extraordinaire Jerry Wexler. In 1968, Aretha's soul-stirring songs led Detroit disc jockey Pervis Spann to anoint her "The Queen of Soul."

Aretha was a staunch supporter of the Civil Rights Movement. She underwrote various civil rights campaigns and events. In 1967, she toured with actors Harry Belafonte and Sidney Poitier to raise money for the Southern Christian Leadership Conference. She also refused to perform for segregated audiences.

Aretha's gift was her ability to take a song and interpret it in such a way that it feels like she wrote it herself or that the song was written for her alone to sing. "(You Make Me Feel Like) A Natural Woman" was tailor-made for her voice. Few people know that Otis Redding wrote and was the first person to record "Respect." After he heard Aretha's version, he smiled and said, "'Ain't no longer my song. From now on, it belongs to her.'" "Respect" is Aretha's most popular and most enduring song. In the 1960s, it was embraced by the Civil Rights Movement as an anthem. Later the women's movement adopted the song as a crowd favorite.

In 1982, Aretha moved back to Detroit to help care for her father, after he was shot twice during a burglary in his Detroit home. Reverend Franklin died in 1984.

Aretha was the first woman inducted into the Rock & Roll Hall of Fame, in 1987, and in 2010, *Rolling Stone* magazine named her the best singer of all time. She won eighteen Grammy Awards and had more than seventy chart-topping songs. These include "Rock Steady," "(You Make Me Feel Like) A Natural Woman," "Do Right Woman–Do Right Man," "Chain of Fools," "Respect," "Think," "Dr. Feelgood," "Day Dreaming," "Call Me," "I Say a Little Prayer," "Freeway of Love," and "Who's Zoomin' Who?" In 1972, Aretha recorded the gospel album *Amazing Grace*, which became the top-selling album of her career. In 2018, *Amazing Grace*, a documentary on the making of the album, was released.

Aretha was married twice. In 1961, she married her first husband, Ted White. White, a Detroit native, was also her manager. The marriage, volatile and difficult, ended in 1969. From 1978 to 1984, she was married to actor Glynn Turman. Aretha had four sons, Clarence, Edward, Ted, and Kecalf.

Aretha received Kennedy Center Honors in 1994 and a

LARRY FRENCH/BET/GETTY IMAGES

Presidential Medal of Freedom, the highest civilian award, in 2005. She was invited to sing at President Bill Clinton's inauguration in 1993. For President Barack Obama's 2009 inauguration, she wore a beautiful and unforgettable heather gray hat with a huge bow and Swarovski crystals.

She worked with a variety of musicians, including George Michael, Michael McDonald, Annie Lennox and the Eurythmics, and Luther Vandross. Franklin maintained her signature singing style as she produced hits with newer artists, such as Lauryn Hill ("A Rose Is Still a Rose") and Fantasia ("Put You Up on Game"). In 2014, she did a soulful rendition of Adele's "Rolling in the Deep."

On August 16, 2018, Aretha Louise Franklin died from pancreatic cancer. Tributes poured in from around the world, and her loss was felt deeply by people across generations. The homegoing service was a star-studded, seven-hour celebration of her life and bold streak across the music world. Family members and friends told stories of her generosity, love, and lifelong support of her hometown of Detroit, especially New Bethel Baptist Church, where she got her singing start all those years ago. New Bethel's pastor Robert Smith Jr. said, "'Countless people have been given hope for life because of her singing, and the way her voice has made every guy and every girl feel like they could make it.'"

In 2019, Aretha was posthumously awarded a Pulitzer Prize, special citation, "for her indelible contribution to American music and culture for more than five decades."

A NOTE FROM THE AUTHOR

I grew up in the late sixties in a home with lots of albums. A few hundred R&B and jazz LPs lined the walls of our Harlem living room. The ones in heavy rotation were spread about on the shag carpet.

My dad was very particular about the record player. I wasn't allowed to touch it. Between his open palms, he'd hold the LP he was going to play next. After he set it carefully on the spindle, he'd say, "Listen here, Tiger" (my nickname). "Check *this* out." One day, in 1967, Dad put on Aretha.

The album he played was *I Never Loved a Man the Way I Love You*. I was transfixed by the cover, a beautiful brown lady adorned with what looked like a dress and earrings made of glass-crystal shells, with a pretty pink background. Her voice, though, is what knocked me out. *I Never Loved a Man the Way I Love You* is filled with wall-to-wall classics, beginning with "Respect."

The title track is the third song in. At six years old, I was a child listening to grown folks' music.

I had no idea what Aretha was singing about. But man, was it exciting. Her voice, the horns, the sighs, those wails, the insistent piano, and the background harmonizing. Aretha sings in vivid detail about the hooks and haunts of love—high drama! We played that album so much the needle started skipping.

Decades later, I still well up when I hear "Natural Woman," that beautiful, redemptive thank-you song. And, I shed tears when I hear "Call Me," with Aretha's urgent pleas for her lover to call the minute he arrives at his destination. The tears come because Aretha's songs have the perfect emotional pitch. The words, the timbre of her voice, the sounds, the silences work your heart over.

Aretha has music for many moods, jubilant, down and out, on the comeback, and triumphant.

I think I'll play my favorite right now. "Dr. Feelgood," anyone? My, my goodness.

A NOTE FROM THE ILLUSTRATOR

What a thrill to be asked to illustrate a picture book about Aretha Franklin, one of my favorite singers growing up! I have been dancing and singing along to Aretha's music for as long as I can remember. I love her voice and her phrasing, her R&B as well as her gospel records, but before starting the book, I knew very little about her life—only her music.

That's why I love illustrating books about real people. I learn so much history while working on them, and I love to research the details of the time periods they encompass: the fashions, the hairstyles, the cars. Aretha's look changed with the times and kept up with fashion. So it was a lot of fun to paint her in the different gowns and hairstyles she wore on stage, and of course I listened to her music for inspiration while I worked on the book!

Even before I started the sketches, I knew that I wanted to make sure I visually acknowledged Aretha as the Queen of Soul, and so I chose royal colors. I used purple and gold in many of the spreads, and I had Aretha wearing gold or yellow in as many illustrations as I could. I even hid crowns on a few of the pages. I also wanted the illustrations to show the emotion and power of Aretha's voice. Her expressions and body language when she was performing only hint at the force that was Aretha. I hope I captured it.

I was still working on the illustrations when Aretha died. I was so sad. I had known she was ill, but I hoped she would get to see the book when it was finished: our tribute to her. I think she would have liked it.

SONGS BY ARETHA FRANKLIN

Aretha Franklin had countless hits over the course of her career, which were included on more than forty albums. Here are some of her most popular songs:

I Never Loved a Man (The Way I Love You) (1967)
Do Right Woman–Do Right Man (1967)
Respect (1967)
Chain of Fools (1967)
Baby I Love You (1967)
(You Make Me Feel Like) A Natural Woman (1967)
Dr. Feelgood (Love Is a Serious Business) (1967)
Think (1968)
(Sweet Sweet Baby) Since You've Been Gone (1968)
Ain't No Way (1968)
I Say a Little Prayer (1968)
Don't Play That Song (1970)

Spirit in the Dark (1970)
Call Me (1970)
Bridge Over Troubled Water (1971)
Oh Me Oh My (I'm a Fool for You Baby) (1971)
Rock Steady (1971)
Spanish Harlem (1971)
Day Dreaming (1972)
Young, Gifted and Black (1972)
Amazing Grace (1972)
Until You Come Back to Me (That's What I'm Gonna Do) (1974)
Something He Can Feel (1976)
Jump to It (1982)
Freeway of Love (1985)
Who's Zoomin' Who? (1985)
A Rose Is Still a Rose (1998)

NOTES FOR "MORE ABOUT THE QUEEN OF SOUL"

"like a fairy-tale princess": David Ritz, *Respect: The Life of Aretha Franklin*, p. 34.

"'She came from a distant musical planet where children'": David Ritz, *Respect: The Life of Aretha Franklin*, p. 31.

"'Ain't no longer my song. From now on, it belongs to her.'": David Ritz, *Respect: The Life of Aretha Franklin*, p. 161.

"'Countless people have been given hope for life'": Adam Graham, "Aretha Franklin: Lifelong Commitment to Detroit," *The Detroit News*, June 21, 2018, https://www.detroitnews.com/story/news/michigan/michiganians-of-year/2018/06/21/aretha-franklin-lifelong-commitment-detroit-michiganian-year-detroit-news-lifetime-achievement-award/720527002/.

"for her indelible contribution": https://pulitzer.org/winners/aretha-franklin.

SOURCES

Franklin, Aretha and David Ritz. *Aretha: From These Roots*. New York: Crown Productions, 1999.

Maraniss, David. "Detroit's Forgotten 'Dream.'" *Washington Post*. June 20, 2013, https://www.washingtonpost.com/opinions/detroits-forgotten-dream/2013/06/20/4ca4b61a-d868-11e2-a9f2-42ee3912ae0e_story.html?utm_term=.30ad2b61238b.

McAvoy, Jim. *Aretha Franklin*. Philadelphia: Chelsea House Publishers, 2002.

Newkirk, Vann R., II. "Aretha Franklin's Revolution." *The Atlantic*. August 16, 2018, https://www.theatlantic.com/entertainment/archive/2018/08/aretha-franklins-revolution/567715/.

Remnick, David. "Soul Survivor: The Revival and Hidden Treasure of Aretha Franklin." *The New Yorker*. March 28, 2016.

Ritz, David. *Respect: The Life of Aretha Franklin*. New York: Little, Brown and Company, 2014.

Rose, Caryn. "Songs of Faith: Aretha Gospel." *Pitchfork*, March 25, 2019, https://pitchfork.com/reviews/albums/aretha-franklin-songs-of-faith-aretha-gospel/.